The Red B

Cindy Harris
Illustrated by Anthony Carnabuci

Rigby®

A Harcourt Achieve Imprint

www.Rigby.com
1-800-531-5015

The red balloons fly
over the park.

3

The red balloons fly
over the hill.

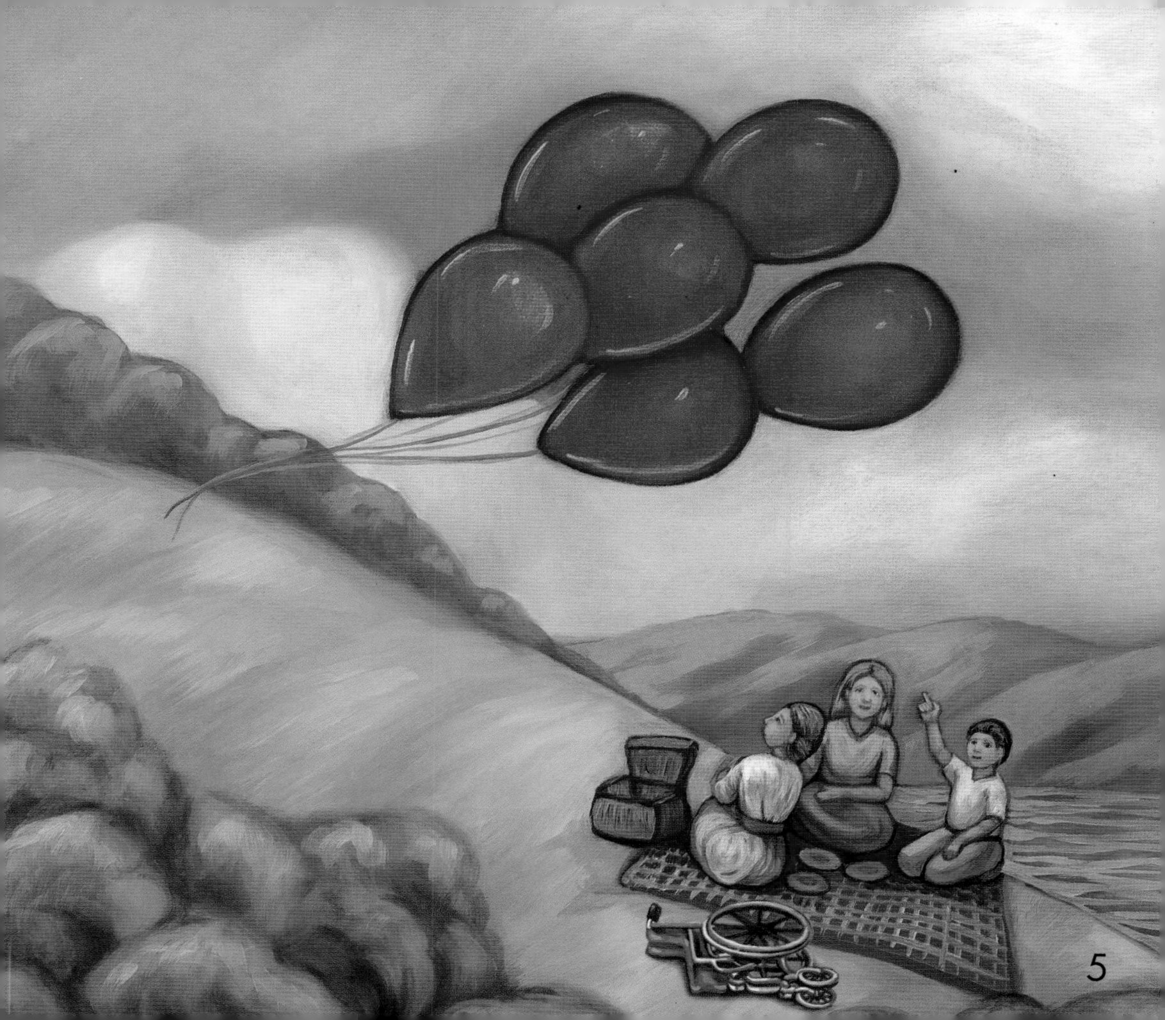

The red balloons fly
over the store.

The red balloons fly
over the school.

9

The red balloons fly
over the water.

The red balloons fly
over the trees.

The red balloons fly
over the house.

The red balloons fly over me!